TWO OF EVERYTHING

TWO OF EVERYTHING

poems

Sally Keith

MILKWEED EDITIONS

Published 2024 by Milkweed Editions
Printed in the United States of America
Cover design by Mary Austin Speaker
Author photo by Abdulrahman Naanseh
24 25 26 27 28   5 4 3 2 1
First Edition

Library of Congress Cataloging-in-Publication Data

Names: Keith, Sally, author.
Title: Two of everything : poems / Sally Keith.
Description: First edition. | Minneapolis, Minnesota : Milkweed Editions, 2024. | Summary: "An abundant and anticipatory collection of poems exploring the season of waiting that precedes adoption"-- Provided by publisher.
Identifiers: LCCN 2023058814 (print) | LCCN 2023058815 (ebook) | ISBN 9781639550944 (trade paperback ; acid-free paper) | ISBN 9781571311535 (ebook)
Subjects: LCSH: Adoption--Poetry. | LCGFT: Poetry.
Classification: LCC PS3561.E3773 T96 2024 (print) | LCC PS3561.E3773 (ebook) | DDC 811/.54--dc23/eng/20240108
LC record available at https://lccn.loc.gov/2023058814
LC ebook record available at https://lccn.loc.gov/2023058815

Milkweed Editions is committed to ecological stewardship. We strive to align our book production practices with this principle, and to reduce the impact of our operations in the environment. We are a member of the Green Press Initiative, a nonprofit coalition of publishers, manufacturers, and authors working to protect the world's endangered forests and conserve natural resources.

for Juana

Contents

"And when we wake up, we have to concede that it's been day all night long, and that everything has kept going on its own. So night is just the beginning of day, as winter is the beginning of the year. And whether one bulb beneath the snow or a child in her bed, the light can always get in, as long as we live. And as long as we live, we can't think it away, either—the light."

—INGER CHRISTENSEN

TWO OF EVERYTHING

What If

Sometimes Amor and I feel like we live on a river
other times we feel stuck.

We have hazy ideas about what we want
and go for long walks by night.

The size of the trees in the neighborhood,
back behind our building, behind the wide avenue
mostly willow oak and maple
make us think of ourselves outside of time.

The lights from the houses and the lights from the streetlamps
do not interrupt the shadows, no,

it happens naturally
that darkness shifts.

*

When Night spoke
it said, *listen*

listen, there is nothing
that will not end—

*

At a certain point Amor says, "You have not written a poem
                 since we've been together"
which is not entirely true
       but neither is it false enough.

Amor, a lover of podcasts,
a lover of stories

occasionally she sits down to supper and sighs.
She thinks I should write more openly about my life.

*

I don't want to feel out of shape.
I don't want to make rules about when I drink.
I don't want to cook anything else.

I did want to see the Vermeer, though we did not.
I wanted to see the Vermeer, but not to imagine
making all that light from the dark.

*

At the top of the stairs in the house. In the house where I grew up
and again that night slept. She stands. She who cannot go up

or down, not anymore. She has a halo and why would she not?
It's not a halo. It's a feeling that cannot fade. It feels like terror.

It feels like love. I think of her nightgown glowing at the edges
as if there were no body inside. But her body is not gone,

not yet. I have never seen a ghost, except
those I have felt inside my dreams

dropping necklaces down lightly onto my neck, touching
the small of my back with a hand. Like that, yes.

Whisper something
I'm listening.

*

Down the street
          a man rolls a mattress
out the front door of his house.

The bushes have grown so thick
          that once he turns the corner
you have no idea

                    what will happen next.

*

On some of the nights
it sounded like poems

inside of what later
I would understand
as the hypnagogic state.

I rode up roads as steep
as my own flexed feet—

whether or not the shortcut
worked, I woke. Waking I

kept hearing one thing
inside of the other.

*

And night says, no.
        It's been ten years
it's been twenty.

It's been five days, no,
        it's been many.

*

"Oh, I thought you were the philosopher," I say,
disappointed,

when Amor comes to bed
after working late.

*

Evidence, the judge explains, is what can be seen. You cannot say
for sure if the man had a knife or not; the knife is not evidence. The
case involved an armed robbery near a convenience store to the east
of where we lived. Most of the transaction had been recorded by a
camera on a lamppost above a four-way stop.

*

Unseen instances saturate a single life.

*

This moss is not the moss
of childhood
when we sat beside the pond
for picnics

the pond forgotten
and afterward
confused with Frost's
spring pool

whereby new leaves
blotted out
what chance there would have been
. . . well, to reflect

this moss appears as though
it might not hold
the bank in place, here
in the sliver

of a park, the one dividing
our neighborhood
from the little commercial
district—

there's just a stream
down here

just a path meandering—
and the stream
an obstacle
and a delight

to cross—

*

I had been dreading jury duty the same way most people dread jury duty. To my surprise, however, I quickly became convinced, not only by the judge, herself, but, if honest, by the commute, the lunch break, the plastic sandwich case I used to prop open my book.

*

Amor, the delicate petals of the lily you bought
have just begun to drop.

*

"Inertia" is the word I keep forgetting I forgot.

*

We bought a king-sized bed
that came in a box

we'd opted for the new possibilities—soft but firm but soft—
and because deflated
                       foam pillows came free

and puffed into shape like—

    like giant loaves of miracle bread
    like magical objects we didn't know to want—

when the obscenity sprung from the box
and learned to relax, we figured

the chemical waft would fade

eventually
eventually

the night would give us
what we want.

*

Double rainbows, two herons.
Sets of twins across the street.

Ode to strangeness,
ode to luck.

Strawberry wallpaper
in my grandparents' house.

"Speedboat, speedboat,
turn on the gas."

Pointing

My mother once cared for a baby whose mother worked full-time
while finishing a degree. One summer the baby went to South
Carolina. When she returned, we were surprised to notice the
difference when she spoke. We were teenagers. What did we expect?
Strangers pointed at my mother and the baby in the grocery store, at
the playground, getting gas. Years later I learned that though adopting
the girl had crossed my mother's mind, more pressing was the clarity
she felt against it. Meanwhile, the girl's mother finished her degree,
got work, got married, and kept the daughter she loved close inside
her own life. A success story, anyone would agree. I don't know where
the girl is now. I doubt she would remember us. I can still see her out
there, walking across the grass.

*

An aster
A stone

The world
A word

A drop
A background

Thought
An aster

A stone
A stone

A bolt
An error

An aster
A flower

The blueness of
The hydrangea bush

*

Amor shares a podcast about a woman who has so many bad things
happen to her, including the upstairs neighbor falling through the
ceiling to her apartment, that you cannot imagine how she will
persist. She persists. Amor shares improbable love stories that finally
work. Podcasts about entrepreneurs, food, scientific facts. Podcasts
about podcasts. I like one in Spanish, or did, though mostly for the
challenge of understanding it. Sometimes together we think about
what it is that makes her love the podcasts and me not. She likes the
company of the stories, while I'd rather be left in empty space.

*

Night said
listen, you

will hear it
when it

comes. Night
said, *listen*

you will hear
when it comes.

*

We were not totally sure what the possibilities were for becoming
lesbian parents. Some of my opinions and some of Amor's opinions
didn't feel safe to repeat. "There are so many options," we both had
heard. We did and did not understand whether there was a wrong or
a right.

*

Place of rest
Symbol of life

An idyllic forest
Makes sense

Place of rest
Do whatever

Symbol of life
Search all over

You can make
What you want

Symbol of life
Place of rest

*

It is what you remember that controls the facts, not the reverse. The judge reminds us, "It is you and you alone . . . yours is the burden of proof." Evidence, the judge explains, is what can be seen. The men and women called to testify may not tell stories; they only answer questions when asked. When the rules of the court are broken, the opposing attorney will object. The judge opens the trial by saying that she may appear to be irritated by the barrage of objections, but that she is not. Looking back, this is a point I very much liked: whether or not she was irritated, she did not want her irritation to affect our judgment and she simply said it. Sometimes language that feels metaphorical is not. We were to tune our attention to just the facts.

*

I'm finishing my novel
sitting in a garden.

For the protagonist's last act
she swallows
a seed.

Did the gecko see?

But for its belly
in and out
unstirring.

How thin the skin.
How minuscule the circuitry.

*

As soon as we move in, as soon as all the boxes from my apartment
and all the boxes from Amor's apartment have been crammed in the
two-bedroom space, we both slump to the floor in relief, except there
is no relief. An older woman, one of the building's many, has just
made casual mention of the impending construction project. *Pointing*
is what she'd said. A construction team, we learn, will arrive and set
up camp behind the building with a large plastic tarp. They will work
in sections. They will blast the mortar from between bricks and fill it
back in. Will this be noisy? Of course. Will there be dust?

*

Yes, dust.
Dust into dust.

*

Amor
A moor

A harbor
A shelter

A home
A house

*

I start reading Darwin, curious
      about the sentences, I guess. I keep on reading

after arriving at the chapter in which Darwin
          decides on different-sized vials

for capturing dust. I mean,
      talk about the smallest little thing

            talk about commitment.

*

Amor suggests that bit about writing and "just showing up." Even if
you are writing a grocery list, she urges, you are writing. As for herself,
Amor has an agent who is waiting for a book, a book that needs to be
read. I cannot help but register the vehemence with which the agent
insists.

*

I decide to play tennis, in part
because I sense it is a metaphor for life.

Bob is always out at the courts.
He hits lobs because they are airy.

Between lobs, therefore,
there is an increased time to think.

He wants to win and reads books on the subject.

*

I want to believe in more than one part of the mind at once.
I want to stop thinking so hard about all the days of my life.

*

For the trial, an extra juror had been chosen in case someone got sick
or didn't show up. At the time, this made perfect sense. We had had
to answer a series of questions before the lawyer selected us. Though I
had answered point-blank, I sensed that when I said "no," they heard
"yes"; my "yes" might also mean "no." I couldn't think fast. Was there
some path available, upon which my fate might have shifted tracks?

*

Our move was a bad idea. From the start.
Our building is draped in plastic sheets.

We are not at all concerned, if honest,
with how much less condensation will creep.

We cannot see the street.
It is extraordinarily hot.

We want to move out. We feel taken.
The signs apologize to the families,

the babies trying to sleep, and the upset pets,
all of which only adds injury to our hurt.

*

The car radio says
someone has stolen
the sketches

from Darwin's notebooks
including the famous
"Tree of Life."

*

Night says
                    I am neither interlocutor
            nor rubicon

                    neither soothsayer
nor psychologist

*

Is this a mother book?
A poet friend asks.

It wasn't but it was.
Was but wasn't.

Dreaming halts
my sink into sleep.

*

One type of story frequently explored in podcasts is the adoption
story. It fits the hope-despair-hope parameter perfectly. More than
most of the podcasts I've heard on the radio, adoption narratives
are just as likely to end badly as they are to end well. Like in real
life, I suspect. The particular podcast I can't shake is told from the
perspective of the birth mother who narrates the visits she has with
her son. The parents who have adopted the boy adhere to the most
so-called ethical of arrangements—visits, letters, photographs—which
the three parents have together set up. When the birth mother visits
her son, she goes on walks with him in the woods behind the family's
house. The producers frame the story using a thwacking sound for
the tree branches snapping back as they pass. The birth mother has
no complaints against the adoptive parents, but, at the same time, she
regrets her decision, all of it, every bit. If I had never heard the podcast,
it is certainly true that I could have also imagined the story, I would
have, in fact, but that's not the point. *Thwack. Thwack.*

*

Once there was a whale
all washed up
on a shore

but when I stopped
to see it close
I found it only metaphor.

The horizon whipped
like a treadle
suddenly there were stars.

Swing swing . . .
my grandmother had sung
and a wall of fire fanned.

Swing for the thicket
Notch for the wind

The wall was all the songs
my grandmother had ever sung.

*

Admittedly, I have been thinking about how occasions might prompt
the writing of a poem—whether wrongly or right— if not also about
the nature of poetry itself. In all the shuffling of drafts, notebooks,
and old files on my laptop, by chance I come across a note on the lyric,
which I have attributed to JL, describing the lyric as an opportunity
to escape the self. Elsewhere, cacti grow like organ pipes.

The grandfather is dancing in the street. Beside enormous rocks,
a guide holds up the paintings he's made to help visualize how the
fragmented images would once have looked. Goodbye, dear friend.
I'm holding onto the potential of song, the skip and lift.

*

Night, the executioner, night
        the judge, night

                the soaker-up-er,
                        night the salve.

*

"Maybe if the child were smart." "Maybe if the child could regularly
take trips back to wherever they were from." "Maybe if the child
were to be procured at birth." "Maybe if they looked *very* different."
"Maybe if they were also white." "Maybe if they had a sibling." "Maybe
if . . . ." "Maybe if . . . "

*

Like fire coming fast down a track.
It is you and you alone
yours is the burden of proof.

Fruitlessness

I want Amor to promise me that everything will be all right.
But she won't.

What if? How come?
She won't say.

She will not say things she does not know.
I get that.

I get that language
has nothing to do with the unfolding
of real-life events.

And yet, I would like
an ounce of comfort.

*

Until the time of deliberation, no one knew which one of the jurors
would be dismissed. We showed up. Old and young, mostly Black
and white, tall and short, professional and not. One wore shoes like
slippers; one brought a dog. One of us wore a floral T-shirt, while
others appeared dressed for work. We went our separate ways during
each of the allotted breaks. What we had in common, had I to guess,
was our curiosity. Who knew what would come next?

*

Night suggests, one day you may love this story.
You really might.

*

Amor explains that sand from the Sahara is blown all the way across
the ocean and turns into dust. There is more of a story, but I don't
remember it. Sometimes my not remembering worries Amor. That she
worries upsets me; not that I don't forget a lot, I do, but I don't think
the things I forget are, like, medically a threat.

*

A stack of paper envelopes

      the bottom creases of which keep the tiny seeds lined up—
carrots, lettuces, squash—

                      and the brown paper bag
          melt into a corrugated mass.

It had stormed and, my fault, yes,
     I left them out. Afterward, because I could not extract

the seeds
        I just threw them out.

*

Listen, you are not connecting the dots
says the tennis coach.

He asks why, *why*, if you have once been great
can you not return to the same place?

Catch your racquet.
Show no emotion.

The form of the stroke must repeat.
It's the creativity I do not like.

*

Has all one could say about Ravel's *Boléro* already been said?
Back and forth forever, back and forth.

*

Must the fertility center
Shady Grove
be named for an idyllic place?

*

Often I have written
in my notebook—
like a prayer to not forget—

the words of Virginia Woolf
when asked about the symbol
of her famous lighthouse

I meant nothing by it.

*

It's after a sonogram and we are looking for jeans in one of those
lower-level, knock-off department store shops where you can have the
dumb pleasure of a cheap pair of fancy socks. Days later, a doctor calls
with results. I am in the gym, up in the padded loft people use for
sit-ups. By the time I understand, I have already sensed the dead end,
even predicted it, and as if to make the doctor feel better, I say "thank
you," quickly adding "I'll stop." The doctor commends my wisdom
and hangs up.

*

By mistake I see the surface of the sun
up close.
The golden-red triangles

bulge on the internet.
Like one of the hedge apples
we used to kick down the street

the tiny segments of sun reverberate
in time-lapse. Of hedge apples
there are people who say

they are magic, though,
seriously, I doubt it.

I turn off the sun
not knowing, otherwise,
what to do with it.

*

"Fruitlessness," says my friend flatly on the phone. "Some people don't
even know it exists." My friend keeps on talking. She is writing a book.
I stare out the window to a patch of Queen Anne's lace, flower my
grandmother loved, flower we picked by the ditches running by her
road, where we walked, where the walk we took we called the walk "to
the persimmon tree" (persimmon the fruit, it's worth mentioning, so
my grandmother said, "to turn your mouth inside out"), where when
night fell we would scoop handfuls of loose pebble, run out, ahead of
the sauntering adults, to throw to the ground with all of our might—
one of the rites of passage, that, throwing the pebble hard enough to
make a spark.

*

The Spanish village
the thin bracelets we bought

a single desk for writing
a single bulb for light

a field
for digging potatoes

you might fry
in a pot.

The child laughed
and rolled
on a cot

You don't even know

the word for sheet
the word for rock.

*

Amor is pouring crepe batter into the pan. The pale pool expands, stiffens just at the edges but the shape won't hold, not yet. She pushes the batter to the side, as one does, crumpling it before moving the mass to a plate. We eat the pieces of rejected crepe. We lean into the corners made of the counter's negative space, one across from the other. Out of sorts, we hold the crepe in our hands, adding butter or whatever else: tiny leftover chicken bits, squares of cheese, and then, one by one, the rest of an old bag of chocolate chips.

*

"Hello, hello" says the lighthouse
in the gorgeous picture book.

*

On my bed I remember you
I think of you through the watches of night.

*

The priest on the podcast reflects:
it is the edges I have sought.

*

Design within Reach. Room and Board. *Dwell. Elle Decor, House Beautiful. Architectural Digest.* We want a new house and collage images of the dreamed-after-house. Sleek sofas that do not sink, pale and polished wooden floors with woolen rugs of bright colors, large abstract art. Tiny animals thoughtfully placed: say, an intricately carved calf under an enormous lamp.

*

An awesome omen
A cipher of stars

A meticulous hedge
A lush heath

An aster, a stone
A rose, a rose—

Our Story

I hear one thing in terms of another.

*

The word, a world.

*

Addressing the back sides of the notebook pages
illegible for all the bleeding ink

Night says, *listen*

these years you press upon
press upon you too much.

*

Amor and I argue over a book I love and she does not. She finds the
scenario banal, maybe even petulant. The main character in the book,
clearly a stand-in for the author, though not marketed as such, has a
child, a husband who makes mistakes, and a generally difficult life. I
suppose this is what you would say the book is about. But the story is
not the glorious part.

*

A fox scuttles across the street at six o'clock on the dot.

*

The ultimate dream is a densely beautiful poem. The notebooks are
the groundwork: the underneath. The notebooks are the fuel but
unlike fuel they consume more energy than they give off.

*

Listen, night repeats.

*

Down Chesapeake, past the row of billion-dollar modernist houses,
across the parkway, and up into the park, I keep trying to look but
everything looks like something else. The park just like the idea of
a park. I'd guess the water is real as it moves fast enough to cause
eddies and look dangerous, but the truant teens eating their bags of
chips reinstate my disbelief. Horses pass. The idea of horses. The path
running alongside the creek has been flattened by the city-folk on
weekend walks. The bark on the trees perfectly smooth to the touch.

*

Listen, says night

                         you will hear it

when it comes

*

Full of notes, recordkeeping (birthdays, weather, deaths, dinner dates), freewriting, and copied-down fragments and sentences from books, when one notebook is filled up, I put it on the shelf. Eventually I recopy the parts I like. Sometimes I record disagreements with Amor, which, while supporting the notion of writing as a form of comfort, I should know well enough to resist. Then again, it can be encouraging to witness in retrospect the conflicts that have resolved into dust.

*

Fox eyes
not diamonds
floating thigh-high

in the oblivion
of a suburban street.

The fox tail
like a fifth appendage
dragged

as another animal
would drag
an injured foot.

*

Forced to wait an extra day for someone to come inspect our
apartment, after which a person from our building must meet the
dog to confirm the dog's new residence, I am unreasonably upset.
This is taking too long. We need her with us. We had wanted a
puppy, but quickly agreed on Rosie—house-trained, no barking,
raised on a farm by three sisters, her only limitation, according to the
profile, concerns playing "dress up." Some say we rescued our dog,
but I am not convinced.

*

Night does not interrupt the day.
Day does not interrupt the night.

*

In a chapter on rhyme in Russian poetry
rhyme is like a motion throwing a poem
out of itself

a meta-real movement
we cannot truly understand in English.

"Love-words" the writer calls
the rhyming pair of Russian words.

Words, like people, go out in search.

*

I think of Hopkins' long lists
the poems he did not write in favor of
his notebooks.

*

Night is
nothing

if not
patient.

Night is
night

is
night.

*

Sound of shuffling paper, sound of constant phone calls which our soon-to-be attorney is obliged to take—she is talking to her intern at the courthouse, continually begging our forgiveness. *It's a messy case* and then she'll add, a little under her breath, *when are they not?*

*

The scales of justice are gold and miniature in a custom-made glass case. It's a home office but something about the setup feels like a model for something else. The repetitive desire we express to do things right, the care to avoid any false step. You might say it feels ridiculous.

*

Between phone calls we are given a hazy purview of the process: we'll list all the states where we have friends so that the part-lawyer, part-matchmaker can look for agencies in states where we would be able to relocate.

*

"Kids are kids" she says when hers appears on the staircase, home from school and sick. We follow her prompts. We tell her "what kind of child" we want. What will we or will we not accept?

*

Thwack. Thwack.

*

Night says, I am an assemblage

      which means there is no discerning

where this began

      where it stops—

*

We drive off in silence, noticing buildings we had not seen before on Georgia Avenue, which we take south to the Library of Congress. The lecture is on the physicality of books. I listen with my skepticism; Amor sketches portraits in her notebook.

*

There is no dissecting

          night from night from night

*

For Rosie, we easily agree to the training classes, the first of which
takes place in a basement near U Street. Gay couples sit sipping beer
in the sun. We walk Rosie in on a rope. A sense faint enough to ignore
taps at the back of my mind. "You know that feeling," the teacher says,
"when you are sitting in your chair, alone, with your dog in a room,
and the dog lifts its head and just gives you a look."

*

Sometimes, it's true, I annoy Amor so much.
I call after the dentist when she is trying to work.

Oh, sing me a song, then, I'll say to myself.

*

A thistle, a key.
A sentence like a street.

A village organized
in tightening rings

as it turns one notch
away from

the sun. Such random
divisible

things.
The purple thistles

filling the field
where a woman walks

digging at a key
in her palm, along

the teeth
of which, she

mindlessly runs
her other thumb

and again
and again.

*

The profile says Rosie is part beagle, which gives us the idea that once off the leash she will run and run and run. People hypothesize that she's part greyhound or whippet because of the way she curls her body up between gaits, tucks her head, and springs. To figure out how fast she *really* is, I buy a line and plan to throw the ball within the circumference allowed by the length, one of those ideas that ends even worse than it ever began.

*

Some say night counters day, as if night
        stood blanketly

                like a half,
a perfect moon-phase, a diagram
        in a math book—

*

The attorney suggests that Amor and I make a postcard of our life.

*

The card should include our picture and what has increasingly come to
be known as "our story." The idea is that someone we know may know
someone, who may know someone who is pregnant and cannot keep
the baby. We can leave them, for example, at tables in restaurants after
we eat. We can hand them to the postman, to the checkout lady, leave
them in stacks wherever we can imagine a pregnant woman might look.

*

Thwack.

*

Our friend arrives with a housewarming gift, a coffee-table book about nests. This is perfect given my scavenging for anything to fill the notebooks, suddenly threatening to go blank. One way I've thought of my habit is that I'm just following the advice they give all "waiting" families: learn a language, to sew, to cook, read great books, get in shape, connect with friends, learn to play chess, a new sport, an instrument. As for the notebooks, there are the months, no years, of the sentence-project: five per day on any topic; there is the Darwin, a collaged abecedarian built from the *Origin of Species* glossary; the eco-doomsday project; the *Paradise Lost*. As for the nests, say what you want, they are such an obvious symbol that it is practically boring to think about. And anyway, Amor and I are not nesting. We know better than that. Tell no one, they say. Keep your expectations low. Don't buy stuff.

*

Night repeats, *listen*.

*

There will be asters
says the woman I pass

and because I mistake
her speaking to me

I query a flower
I've always liked

the one by the trellis
but only to discover

it is silk
which the woman
reiterates

with a rudely emphatic
"fake."

*

We keep on telling "our story" in the form of a book, in the form
of multiple-books: handmade books with decorative construction-
paper cutouts, computer-made books, books in Spanish, in English,
books with photographs of our families, our friends, our trips, our
apartment, our dog, our neighborhood . . . our matching blue shirts,
our too-tall bookshelf, our favorite soup, the burlap bag of salt we
brought back from our trip. We tell our story. We tell it again. We get
good at this rendition of ourselves.

Unfinished Abecedarian

*

A

for animal
little animalcule . . .
ammonites, annelids

for articulata
in taxonomy-talk
a joint or a hinge

(I got sucked in
studying all sorts of
stuff, like dust)

for an animal
with partitions
waved in patterns

waves, waves
on waves.

*

Adoption, transracial adoption, adopting in under a year, affordable
adoption, ethical adoption, postpartum and adoption, adoption
and sex, legal logistics, international adoption, breastfeeding and
adoption, lesbian moms, birth moms, first moms, abuse. The subject

matters range. We attend roundtables, webinars, online courses, workshops, weekend conferences. We read books. Sometimes we sit at home and watch the videos online and drink scotch, which seems to not at all impede our ability to pass the required chapter tests. We rack up certificates.

*

1. Brian says some projects are like being in a cul-de-sac and you need to find your way back.

2. My fantasies do, or do not, relate to justice, I think to myself.

3. When she wasn't writing, in the most recent bout of not writing, she lived in a village and it was incredibly, even dangerously, hot.

4. Considering change, a stone is ample proof.

5. The bees are dying, Amor says, the bees are dying again.

*

A hummingbird may pollinate as many as one thousand flowers a day; it lays an egg the size of a bean.

*

We hear about a man in Mayville, by all accounts either the best or the worst. We drive over for an interview. How could this hurt?

"Why aren't you married," he repeatedly asks.

Is he acting or not?
I try to guess what Amor thinks.

*

The man confesses that he likes to work with gay couples (or does he say "help") and because he requires straight couples to be married, he feels it is time, now that gay marriage is legal, to interrogate.

This logic—which does not include the history of gay marriage, the newness of gay marriage or the validity of a gay couple who fundamentally refuses the institution of marriage—he drops, in favor of the narration of his own enormous wedding, a wedding, he is proud to add, he demanded of his spouse.

*

A hot-air balloon for the honeymoon escape, more roses, color pink, than you could imagine, long tables of pink champagne to match, and all of this atop a hill in Mayville, the middle of a totally green lusciousness. Never mind the rest.

*

It must have been that Amor's short hair gave him the idea that she was the man and, therefore, the one who should ask. In general, this kind of thinking is indicative of the way the guy thought. *Evidence is what can be seen.* Applying "the man" and "the woman" to our relationship has never been a help. At the end of our meeting, the man gets very close to Amor's face, lowers one of his hands onto her knee, piles the other hand on top, presses a bit, as one does to make a point: "What if I told you to get down on your knee and propose, right now!" Needless to say, she does not.

*

Night repeats and repeats—

*

The African palm swift uses glue from its gland to stick together a tiny nest, a project that can take as long as four months.

*

1. Sometimes I do think less about babies and birth announcements, but other times pictures on the internet work like evidence: thinking less will not suffice.

2. "He who thinks loses" is the literal translation of the phrase Amor uses to remind me: stop overthinking it.

3. In Jabés' *Book of Questions* I come across a perfect sentence: "To be two means being day, which is formed by morning and night."

4. "Faint or Fly" says the marquee.

5. In Spain, it was so hot that going to buy groceries was out of the question; rather, they said, pull the blinds, stay inside, wait for the dark of night.

*

The Altamira Oriole weaves the nest like a bag—of straw, wool, horsehair, and feather—down through which she will climb to nurture her babies at the base.

*

Amor and I go out on a date. Having arrived at the theater, we take our seats. We know the troupe we've come to see is not a professional troupe and though, sure, it is good to sit in the dark together and watch, we find it quite surprising, even unnerving, how the ballerinas appear so difficult to lift.

*

Whenever my mother got home from traveling someplace far off, she would resolve to greet everyone in the street and in the shops. She was determined to not say "thank you" when she really meant "you're welcome" or "please" or "I'm sorry" or "hey, stop."

*

Reading José Emilio Pacheco's "El Pulpo"
picking out the "o"s—
Helecho, Hongo, Jacinto—

a fern, a fungus, a hyacinth—
which in English disappear
I begin to suppose it's possible to feel an image

here the octopus
that dark god . . . between rocks no one has seen
while harboring the sounds
underneath.

*

I dream we adopt several oversized children.

*

I dream I am going to have a baby and then I wake up.

*

I dream I have a baby the head of which I eat.

*

Thinking back, now, to the time before the jury was adjourned to finally deliberate, the time the number of the extra juror's seat was announced, I recall that the idea of an extra juror I had held in my head like a ghost. When suddenly, to my relief, to my disappointment, mine was the seat announced, I got up and left, depositing in the trash, as instructed, my notebook, my notebook with all my notes.

*

C

for a cutaneous surface
a fat cotyledon

the ever-forking idea
of what was once

for crustaceans
cephalopods

the hairless Cetacea,
blowholes for breathing—

behind one cave
another

someone
spelunking—

(did you read that
too?)

for curculio

sweet beetle
of the weevil family.

*

The bank swallow nests in tunnels of sand and never returns to one it
has used.

*

I am teaching when my phone starts to buzz in my pocket. There is
a baby in California who may or may not need to be adopted. Are
we interested? Are there health concerns? Yes. Are there concerns
about the mother and father? Yes. Yes, the situation could end up
dangerous. There might be a chase. Then, like magic, the possibility
dissolves. This is immediately after we have finished all the paperwork
and are anxious to start. You will rush, the social worker says, rush and
rush, to wait, an idea I hadn't thought of before but soon cannot stop
imagining.

*

Do you ever think about actually *having* a baby?
is a question we are often asked.

*

The dream babies are cylinders, hot-dog-in-a-bun shape.
Arranged in a pyramid, they have been wrapped in mini-blankets,
pink on the left, blue on the right.

*

In line to pick up my long-anticipated child
I dream I'm handed a sandwich-sized plastic bag
filled halfway up with sand.

*

The child is so real in my dream that I call it *you*.
You look like me.

We're sitting together as I brush your sticky bangs back
away from your face.

*

1. Little glitch, I carry it.

2. I like the late Jarabe de Palo song in which the singer, repeating
    "hoy," says, hey, I'm in a bad mood today, sorry.

3. "Night is to day /as half a cold pie is /to the cold tin plate" is the kind of sentence I'd want to lineate; you can't not feel the parts of it.

4. When the vase we loved breaks, we try to hear its directive to loosen our grip.

5. Even if you don't go for astrology, rising and falling signs, color theory, or, really, any of that, when someone suggests your element is fire, it does have an impact.

*

In some scenarios
you may choose

the amount of light
you can tolerate.

The same can be said
of the dark.

*

Sometimes we cry watching documentaries about children trying to connect with their birth parents. We begin to feel, increasingly, if I can just say it, ashamed of ourselves. *Dear judge, are we wrong or right?* Although we feel grateful for exposure to the difficulty of all adoption stories, we do not know what to do. We argue more. We say, fine. Fine then, let's just stop. And we may. We might.

*

F

for flora, fauna
the leaves in the yellow-
green-florescent phase

that part of fall
fat with color

for fossiliferous, furcula
and fossorial

for the soft-bodied
who need to burrow

for feldspars
mineral-forming rocks, rocks
jutting out so

they are graspable or might be

otherwise they dust
invisibly the ground

for feelers
the Latin name for which

I cannot figure—

Sand from the Sahara

Missing you
sometimes I

remember.
I remember

your hands
take my hands,

put one inside
the other. I

can feel
myself

my life
watching.

*

1. One of the ideas I have is naming the puppy Happy, after the
   mother of a child I knew, named Sally—so long ago—but there's
   more to it, of course.

2. Sitting on a hill in Virginia, "This is so exotic," says a friend to the
   wine with a nose of metallic.

3. Alstroemeria is the name of the Colombian flower Amor loves,
   the flower we used in the restaurant where I worked with Marcus,
   the head waiter who got his young girlfriend pregnant.

4. Would the best version of a story include all the beginnings and all the endings or would including everything negate what a story is supposed to be?

5. Little repeated scene, little repeated scene, let's do the day again, please, come back.

*

One day we see the kids' book that tells the story of two penguins who take care of a baby they did not birth. That I'm anthropomorphizing already is obvious. The two penguins are the same sex. You know that, or surely you would have guessed? "Penguins are so gay," Amor tells me, which makes me laugh. Now that gay couples in the United States can marry, we observe, shouldn't we? Or would we? Whom should we ask? The social worker said not to get married, not during "the process." There could be a state or a country that does not allow adoption for gay couples and although they can fix the paperwork so that we appear as roommates, this will take more time. To say we are not fond of this plan is an understatement—not the time, nor the deceit.

*

The therapist says, "There's nothing wrong with fantasy.
Why would there be?"

When I can't write, Amor suggests:
"See a hypnotist."

*

Night says, I am the needle and you are the thread.

*

"There is so much going on with biology"
the barista relays to her friend

considering the bad luck
of an animal going extinct

the moment you decide
to study it.

*

Although I enjoy the idea of *thrifting*, if honest, I hate digging around
in old stuff. I can't be bothered with the idea of a "diamond in the
rough." I know this sounds bad. I do not want to do any more harm to
the earth. I get it, yes: cliché, overstatement, ridiculous, meaningless.
Not that it would change much, but I have wondered if my bad
attitude could be an inherited stance, something innate? My mother,
I remember, was also like this. Let's forget it. Amor, I say, let's catch
a train to the far reaches of the city and share a drink. Let's go to the
countryside, Amor, let's go walk on the puffy, still-green grass.

*

M

for mother
Mammalia

the mammiferous
suckling their young

for a species of spider
a man found in Morocco

(out one night he just saw it
carried it home on his hand)

for Mother's Day
marriage
mammograms:

some secrets, the MD said
are too close
for our good—

*

Searching on the internet, the keyword "alternative" mostly avoids
what we can't afford. I try meteorite rings, rings from wood, rings
using kintsugi. Maybe fulgurites? Something fixed, something
struck by light. There is this one site with eco-friendly rings made

from recycled gold. Amor would love this. Simultaneously, and unbeknownst to me, Amor has found a Dutch artist who cuts three-dimensional birds from glass.

*

Can I just say it?
   Part of me believed
what I wanted
   would be placed
in my lap.

*

A thread
A jot

A grain
A whit

*

My friend gets an order of "cease and desist" after a once-friend recognizes himself in her book. We spend a conversation feeling mad and not mad about this. In the end, she worries, but stands with her description of the guy's obnoxious laugh.

*

It was my birthday
the night I woke
to the square of light.

That's when it happened.
Night spoke—

*

In my inbox there is an email from the fertility center apologizing for
an email, a Valentine's message for new mothers, which they have sent
erroneously to the non-mother group. Yes, I should have erased my
name. Even a long time ago I knew better than to stay on the list. Still,
I could only ever be my unrelenting self.

*

Between dust
more

particles of
dust, no,

no connection
to rust. Rust

is just
old evidence.

*

The hat shop, the lost parrot, the long walk.

The time the woman looks out the window and we know
that whatever she sees stands in for the state of her inner life.

I find years' worth of notes after reading Elizabeth Bowen.

In a series titled "Draft," I try translating Bowen's prose into verse
not the narrative, but the feeling of it.

I imagine shrinking down to walk in a dollhouse—
the plastic ham alongside a miniature carving knife

the teensy weave of a cotton sock
the smallest ever toothbrush.

But nothing feels infinite.

*

The red bird makes a veritable statue of the ring, its nest.

*

There has arrived a photograph in our inboxes. Less the faces of the
young couple, more the way they have positioned themselves for the
selfie. They stare up at the camera-eye looking something between
plaintive and matter-of-fact. You can almost hear the sigh after the
camera clicks, the *there-we-did-it*. The couple has just had a baby and
again find themselves pregnant. They want to make a better life, they
write. By "better" we are not equipped to judge but we do, filling in
all the ways we want to believe two people would do what is right.

*

An order
An everlastingness

*

Yes—

Angel

Baby in a basket; baby in the NICU; baby on the border with the
parents in a fight; baby with an incarcerated father, also a chef; baby
to be born in withdrawal; baby of abuse; baby of incest; baby whose
Indigenous family members will make a final decision six months after
the baby has been placed; baby of a florist; baby of a priest; baby of
the forty-year-old, single white woman with too many other babies to
mother who says, now, yes, with this one, no, no, she just can't.

*

Dear Judge—
Thwack, thwack.

*

A wooden raft
A trilobite

A willow, a pillar
A poplar by water

The hedge, the grit
The feed, the dark

*

1. In this waiting room, they do not play CNN but rather a video with waves crashing repetitively under the ocher sunset.

2. Candlelight or lamplight, which do you prefer?

3. The weight of the moth is relative to the petal upon which it stops.

4. In Dan's book he mentions a few times the debacle of the lyric poet: an inner and an outer life, at once.

5. *Mirror, mirror* everywhere.

*

If it isn't the wind moving the tin can down the street,
what is it?

*

Four ways to specify the person you are going to meet, the Spanish teacher explains: the meeting is by coincidence, the meeting is for the first time, the meeting is to see an old friend, or the meeting is one in which two people travel from different points—a reunion of sorts. I keep confusing the verbs when I practice, in particular when I want to tell stories in the past tense. One idea, the teacher suggests, is that the *meeting* idea be altogether cut.

*

Sac, halo, Bubble Wrap.
Thistle, comb, column, rod.

*

What for?
How come?
What if?

*

If we had been together longer?

If we were married and had honeymoon pictures,
pictures at the altar, pictures feeding one another cake?

If we were straight? If we had a house
not a rented apartment on a busy street?

If we had a photograph of the nursery, walls stenciled,
a crib, a mobile, stuffed animals, doll babies,

etcetera, etcetera
non-gendered colors, an eco-friendly vacation hut,

real art . . .
If—

*

Thwack.

*

A poet I admire asks
"What do you fear the most in your poems?"

Before I feel able to answer,
he answers himself:

"I fear the frivolous."

*

~~DRAFT~~

~~A daguerreotype and lavender soap.~~
~~Half a roasted acorn squash.~~

~~I couldn't sleep, got up while it was dark.~~
~~The couple talked about a ghost.~~

~~A dovetailing, a stretching out of life.~~

~~I made the squash, left you the larger half.~~
~~Objects not symbols.~~
~~I thought to myself.~~

*

The man on the podcast, to me, sounds Spanish,
but really he's Swiss.

*

New tennis shoes are waiting at the door in a box. Not wearing
sneakers with holes rubbed into the soles feels like more of a relief
than it really is, but perhaps only because I hadn't been expecting
them to arrive. I sit to lace the shoes before heading to meet Bob at
the court.

*

Ode to strangeness.
Ode to luck.

*

Outside, the barn owl's soft hiss.

*

The mother in Reno is not open to gay couples and so, no,
she did not choose us.

There will be more mothers, mothers with names like Hope,
mothers like Angel, mothers with names
like Providence.

*

Tonight
          a shape is
chasing
          a shape
in between
          endlessness
like night on
          more night

*

Angel is in perfect condition. Angel does not drink, nor does she do
drugs. Her cause is gay rights. We learn she likes poetry and music.
Though the coincidences verge on comic, Angel is heaven-sent. She
says loyalty is stronger than blood.

*

Night says look
you know this

as darkness cedes
to morning

the snowflakes' drift
is unmappable

uncanny
like dust

an aftermath
cold evidence

*

The Darwin project is a dead-end and on many fronts. And yet. The dutiful part of me (*juiciosa,* Amor says, which, for its proximity to *judicious,* always throws me off) wants to divide the rest of the pages by the remaining number of days in the month and knock it off.

*

I google "baby at six weeks"
to picture

what our angel-baby
will be like

this summer, celebrating
my father's seventieth

sitting up, smiling
a rattle in her mighty grip.

*

I will change

      my life said night

speaking like a circle

      starting the same

place it ends *I*

      will change

my life

*

I had not yet come close

to gathering my thoughts on "Marriage"
the brilliant long scrutiny by Marianne Moore

when there I found myself at one side of the priest
holding onto the hands of Amor.

*

The child in the apartment above us drops his blocks.
The drain on the slender balcony clogs
flooding the sunroom, my bookshelf, my desk.

*

The voice on the Spanish learning app asks
"Can you love two people at once?"

*

Mother, father, husband, wife
He, she, it, they

*

Why do we get what we want in life?
Why do some parts of youth have to fade?

*

Angel writes to say no.
Angel does not choose us.

*

Mother of God. Angel mother. Mother Hen. Mother Nature. Mother
Love. Mama Mía. Mother Teresa. Earth Mother. Mother ship.
Mother of invention. Honor thy. Mamma Bear. Den mother. Mother
board. Board Mother. Soccer Mom. *Mother,* my grandfather would
call to my grandmother. "The Mother." A mother book. Don't say
mamacita. Don't say mother F*cker. Mother humper. Mother mine.
Mama. Mamá. Oma. Mami. Ma. Mom.

Short Fiction

In the first drafts of "our story" the social worker writes back
to explain that these narratives are meant for the mothers, not
academics, a bit of criticism that falls exactly no distance short of
shame and insult. The social worker cannot do enough to make us
understand that "our story" is not really for us. Sometimes a mother
will pick families who have pictures of themselves in matching
pajamas at Christmas, some women might like biking, plants, to
cook or not to cook. It depends on their experience, not ours. This
is not the only time in life I've felt how badly we need practice
understanding this.

*

Amor—
Amor

Harbor, shelter
Home, house

*

"Poetry like mist intrigued me" I struck
      from a draft I'm convinced
shall not, as in *never*, be finished

including the memory of a walk
      behind Napoleon's summer palace

waiting for my ex, for whom I would or would not
        move to France.

At the end, having transposed myself
        to the man in a story I'd read, I find
a silver thermos
        in a stream and pick it up.

"Little tin container of nothingness."

*

Happenstance. Prayer.
Superstition. Coin toss.

Double rainbows. Two herons.
Sets of twins across the street.

Abundantly clear
Amor's message

Please. Stop.

*

1.   Darwin is on the *Beagle* collecting dust.

2.   Rereading the sentences in the notebooks reminds me of looking
    for anything in a secondhand store, a junk shop, or a store of
    antiques.

3. I used to walk in the woods with the girl, Sally, whose mother, like mine, died too young, all out of sequence.

4. As the sky darkens and rain starts, a bee taps at the sliding door as it completes each less than perfect square shape.

5. Was it before or after the hedge trimming, I noticed the blue robin egg in the nest and no mother-bird flying back?

*

My sister texts to see if I remember
the sticker on the mirror
where we used to get our hair cut.

Beautician, not Magician
I text back pretty fast.

Total Concept
one of many Korean-owned shops
near our house

where my mother
ogled hanboks threatening
to buy one

but for our begging her
to not.
Please. Not.

*

Some mothers don't speak English; some make it clear that they
never ever want to be in touch; some have too many other children;
some have been in foster homes; many have not; some mothers want
to name their child; some want a say in the naming of the child and,
minimally, it is respectful to ask; some mothers might want to nurse;
some want photographs and letters, others FaceTime dates; some of
the mothers want regularly scheduled *real* visits; some do not make
it clear what they want; with none of the mothers are we confident
that we connect, though we hope; some mothers will want to mother;
some mothers will wait to decide what they want; all mothers will
change; all mothers change; we practice expecting the obvious.

*

We say "yes."
        She says "no."

Yes, No.
        Yes, No.

Night says, *wait.*
        Amor says, *stop.*

As in
        no, no más.

*

The poem a student turns in charges her mothers with giving her childhood a price. She is adopted. Her anger I can't completely understand, by which I mean I cannot see all the sides of it. I can only see her through what she writes.

*

I imagine language metaphorical changing straight away into fact.

*

Poetry like mist.

*

It isn't the mothers themselves who write. The social worker mediates, sends excerpts. The social worker, we have been made to understand, should already have counseled the mother, putting her interests first. The first mother, the birth mother, should always mother, if at all possible. The pregnancy should be well past the first trimester. The agency will be a permanent resource. We accept this without evidence. We want to feel good about the process. The emails include as much information as possible. "BM in Dubuque, Jennifer due 9/14 with 1/2 Caucasian, 1/2 Hispanic male" reads one subject line. Occasionally, in part of the message, if not through a separate phone call, the social worker will relay her own sense of the story, a sense that translates the recorded story into what can be better understood by knowing a person in real life.

*

Night
in the future

cannot be
night

in the past
or

am I
wrong

is night
uniquely

continuous—

*

Please consider us, we write,
having been asked this time

to extend to the mother
a personal note.

*

We pack for a summer trip, buoyed, and saying nothing about it.

*

"Think, if you can,
about enjoying the moment."

The tennis coach makes a halolike shape
high above his head and glances up.

*

Night says, there is writing on the wall but you cannot see it,
                using an old trope.

*

As we drive the Hudson Valley
the permeable sense
of the river, invisible as it is
runs right there beside us.

*

Night does and does not really speak.

                          Even you know this.

*

"The number of women in the room darken it like trees in a wood"
is a descriptive sentence, context unnecessary, a sentence centered
around a simile-based image, a sentence I had written and loved, until
looking back through my notebook I realize I have stolen it from the
stories of Elizabeth Bowen.

*

We cannot move far enough away from what we want.

*

In memory there is no space between hearing the chime and opening
the message. We are standing under a small window, full of light. We
have barely begun to read when the answer is apparent. This time we
also receive a personal note. The mother has enjoyed our profile and
is sure we will "get picked" soon. But no. The presumption of this
mother reading our fate, an idea I spend my life trying to resist, sends
me off. I beg Amor to call the social worker, which she does, to my

surprise and love and delight. Why? Why? Why? We both want to
know. All the social worker says is *wait*.

*

The arctic underwater spider
on the internet
before I fall asleep is ghostly white.

It does not so much as breathe, I learn,
for technically it can't.
It activates
long slim muscles lining the legs.

The photographer says he has come to love it
swimming there
underneath the earth.

*

[DRAFT]

Of the two boys,
the near hallucination of the weaker

night coming on—
with our awareness

~~they are lost—plays against~~
~~the fantasy. At last,~~

~~when they get inside the little house~~
~~they will understand domestic life.~~

*

I come across a reflection in my notebook, worrying over an exchange I'd had with a student. Unsure how to best support the anger in her poem, I'd suggested revising out the adjective "white" for the women on the plane-ride home from Korea, holding babies on their laps. Wouldn't naming the adoptive mothers' race make the anger stand out? Then again, her anger was right. I knew that. I must have gotten too steeped in my own thoughts. Had I or hadn't I made a mistake?

*

Whisper something to me.
I'm listening. Tell me what it is
you really want.

*

　　　　　Venice like an afternoon on the quay
like wine in paper cups, where we took great trouble
　　　　to find the warehouse in Murano

where a team of Dutch glassblowers had put
an enormous bird, a bird we had even already seen
pump its big glass wings

on the internet, though still we wanted
to see the wings in real life.
Amor like Venice which is

to say love like swirling
all you cannot know
inside a single fingertip.

*

The lake is dark gray and the wind is sharp. A few cousins sit in the
boat in brightly colored coats. It's late summer. We've made a video
to surprise my father on his birthday, or, really, Amor has, splicing
moments of silent film from all the boxes on boxes of film we've paid
to convert. I will and will not remember the video, just as I do and do
not remember the moments the film has caught: the kite, the Mary
Janes, the bathing suit. What I see for the first time in decades will not
change the story I use to describe my life.

*

Scrim, paraffin
Weft, waft
Deliquescent stuff—

*

Sometimes when I tell Amor a thing
I have been thinking,

she gives me this perfect look—

*

Swimming with a mind to forget
when somewhere

unbeknownst
to us

the chime goes off.

Song for the Tulip Tree

If you contain the blood of the saints
and know the truth of our technology

with all your orange hearts
with all your heart-shaped seeds,

if you are a boat
come down and carry me—

and streams sunk deeper behind the stones
and a painting occurred from the dark in my mind.

I cut a piece of root
then, for I knew—

her name would be Providence—

should I mention I was alone, then
should I mention the twin sons I would have

their tiny matching hands.

December Light

Sometimes we read stories backward
to enhance the fate effect.

*

I leave Darwin where I found him, a shape in a shape

*

and pick up *Paradise Lost*.

*

Night and day, light and dark

*

why would anything appear exact?

*

Old road, crewelwork cape, heap on heap

*

note, weed, constellation-shape.

*

Bear, knot, oak leaf, boat

*

a gutter nailed on the side of a house

*

jars on jars

*

seeds, shelves of seeds, seeds where books should be

*

the rungs on the ladders, up and up.

*

Wary, we message back and forth with Providence.

*

The "flic-flac" spider named for the flip
it can do most anywhere to escape.

*

Forget craft, forget learning, reading *Paradise Lost*
I can just barely hold on to the characters

*

and whatever it is they want.

*

Today, tomorrow, next week, a house, a home, a home, a life.

*

The world was all before them, where to choose
their place of rest, and Providence their guide.

*

Two of one thing, two of another.

*

They hand in hand with wandering steps and slow,
Through Eden took their solitary way.

*

We washed our hands.

*

The world went out.

*

We held two tiny heads
right up against our hearts.

*

Earth stood hard as iron/Water like a stone
Snow had fallen/Snow on snow on snow

*

Where flat the winter light awaits—

*

Listen—

*

You know those strange few seconds

*

between the stuff of day and the longed after

*

nothingness of night

*

Amor—

*

Might song approach real life—

*

Goosey, goosey gander
wither wilt thou
wander.

*

And night spoke

*

Listen,
there is nothing

*

that will not end—

Acknowledgments

Thank you to *Inner Forest Service* and *Interim*, where sections of this sequence first appeared, sometimes in different versions. Many of these poems were written with the support of money and time, from George Mason University and the John Simon Guggenheim Memorial Foundation, for which I am very grateful.

My gratitude to everyone at Milkweed.

Thanks to my family and friends for their support and guidance during the writing of this book, and with great love for the two who have so rearranged my day and night.

SALLY KEITH is the author of *Two of Everything*, as well as four previous collections of poetry, including *River House* and *The Fact of the Matter*. Recipient of a Guggenheim Fellowship, she is a member of the MFA faculty at George Mason University and lives in Fairfax, Virginia.

milkweed
EDITIONS

Founded as a nonprofit organization in 1980, Milkweed
Editions is an independent publisher. Our mission is to
identify, nurture, and publish transformative literature and
build an engaged community around it.

Milkweed Editions is based in Bdé Óta Othúŋwe
(Minneapolis) within Mní Sota Makhóčhe, the traditional
homeland of the Dakhóta people. Residing here since time
immemorial, Dakhóta people still call Mní Sota Makhóčhe
home, with four federally recognized Dakhóta nations and
many more Dakhóta people residing in what is now the state
of Minnesota. Due to continued legacies of colonization,
genocide, and forced removal, generations of Dakhóta
people remain disenfranchised from their traditional
homeland. Presently, Mní Sota Makhóčhe has become a
refuge and home for many Indigenous nations and peoples,
including seven federally recognized Ojibwe nations. We
humbly encourage our readers to reflect upon the historical
legacies held in the lands they occupy.

milkweed.org

Milkweed Editions, an independent nonprofit literary publisher, gratefully acknowledges sustaining support from our board of directors, the McKnight Foundation, the National Endowment for the Arts, and many generous contributions from foundations, corporations, and thousands of individuals—our readers. This activity is made possible by the voters of Minnesota through a Minnesota State Arts Board Operating Support grant, thanks to a legislative appropriation from the arts and cultural heritage fund.

Interior design by Mary Austin Speaker
Typeset in Garamond Premier Pro

Adobe Garamond is based upon the typefaces first created by
Parisian printer Claude Garamond in the sixteenth century.
Garamond based his typeface on the handwriting of Angelo
Vergecio, librarian to King Francis I. The font's slenderness makes it
one of the most eco-friendly typefaces available because it uses less
ink than similar faces. Robert Slimbach created a digital version of
Garamond for Adobe in 1989 and his font has become one of the
most widely used typefaces in print.